Post Malone

POST

The Rockstar of a New
Generation
How a Genre-Bending Artist
Redefined Modern Music.

James C. Oliver

TABLE OF CONTENTS

INTRODUCTION

In a world where music genres once
defined artists and their careers, Post
Malone has emerged as a boundary
breaking figure who refuses to be
confined to a single category. His
ability to blend hip-hop, rock, pop and
even country into a sound that is
uniquely his own has made him one of
the most influential and innovative

artists of the 21st century. With his tattoos, laid-back persona, and infectious hits, Post Malone has captured the attention of millions, transcending the typical image of a pop or rap star.

Born Austin Richard Post in Syracuse, New York, and raised in Grapevine, Texas, Post Malone's rise to fame was anything but conventional. From playing guitar in local bands to uploading music on SoundCloud, he was an artist who carved out his path, driven by his love for music and an unshakeable belief in himself. His breakout single "White Iverson," a tribute to the legendary basketball player Allen Iverson, became a viral sensation seemingly overnight, catapulting him from a virtual unknown to one of the most talked-about artists in the industry.

Since then, Post Malone has taken the music world by storm. His albums Stoney, Beerbongs & Bentleys, and Hollywood's Bleeding have topped charts, shattered streaming records and won over critics and fans alike. His tracks, such as "Rockstar," "Circles" and "Sunflower," became anthems that dominated airwaves and playlists, showcasing his versatility as both a singer and songwriter. But beyond the music, Post Malone's influence extends into fashion, social media and the broader cultural landscape. He represents a new kind of artist: one who effortlessly fuses genres, defies expectations and embraces authenticity above all.

This book delves into the life and career of Post Malone, exploring his early beginnings, meteoric rise to fame and the impact he's had on modern music and culture. Through interviews, personal anecdotes, and insights into his creative process, we'll uncover the story of a true rockstar who's reshaping the musical landscape. From his breakthrough hits to his status as an icon for a new generation, this is the story of Post Malone an artist who redefined what it means to be a musician in today's world.

CHAPTER 1: EARLY LIFE AND BACKGROUND

Post Malone was born Austin Richard Post on July 4, 1995, in Syracuse, New York. From an early age, he was surrounded by music and culture, thanks to his father, Rich Post. Rich worked as a DJ in his younger years, exposing young Austin to a wide variety of music, from classic rock to hip-hop. This early exposure laid the foundation for Post Malone's eclectic taste and interest in blending genres, something that would become his trademark as an artist.

Post's childhood in Syracuse was relatively modest. While not growing up in a particularly wealthy or famous family, Austin experienced a supportive environment where his creativity could flourish. His father's vast music collection introduced him to the likes of Bob Dylan, Fleetwood Mac, and 50 Cent, giving Austin a diverse musical palette to draw inspiration from. This exposure to different styles and sounds helped shape the musician he would eventually become.

Family and Early Musical Influences

Though he is often seen as a self-made star, Post Malone's family played a significant role in nurturing his artistic side. His stepmother, Jodie, and father provided him with the tools and encouragement to explore his passions.

Whether it was playing video games, sports, or creating music, Austin's parents made sure to support his wide range of interests. This encouragement was crucial in helping him build confidence and independence.

In his early teens, Austin began to explore playing instruments. He picked up the guitar after being inspired by the popular video game Guitar Hero, which helped fuel his interest in rock music. His initial influences were largely rock-based, with artists like AC/DC, Metallica, and Guns N' Roses taking center stage in his early playing. However, Austin was also fascinated by hip-hop, a genre that was growing in popularity during his teenage years. This mix of rock and hip-hop would later become a defining feature of his sound.

Austin attended Tarrant County College briefly after high school but dropped out to pursue music full-time. This decision, though risky, showcased his determination to follow his passion, even when the path forward wasn't entirely clear. His early years were marked by trial and error, experimenting with different styles and sounds, and trying to find his unique voice in the crowded music landscape.

CHAPTER 2: THE MOVE TO TEXAS AND HIGH SCHOOL YEARS

Life in Grapevine, Texas

When Malone was nine years old, his family relocated from Syracuse, New York, to Grapevine, Texas. This move was due to his father securing a job with the Dallas Cowboys as the assistant director of food and beverage, a position that allowed the Post family a comfortable lifestyle. The shift from the Northeast to Texas was a major change for young Austin. Grapevine, a suburb of the Dallas-Fort Worth metropolitan area, offered a different environment, with a more laid-back atmosphere compared to the hustle and bustle of New York. It was in Texas where Malone would come of age, exploring his talents and navigating the challenges of adolescence.

The influence of Texas on Malone's musical development was undeniable. The state's diverse music scene, from country to southern rock and hip-hop, broadened his horizons even further. Grapevine might not have been a

major music hub, but it provided a
space for Austin to develop his talents
away from the pressures of a big city.
He became increasingly involved in
music, honing his skills and
discovering that music could be more
than just a hobby, it could be a career.

Discovering Music and First Attempts at Songwriting

As Austin transitioned into his teenage
years, his interest in music intensified.
His love for Guitar Hero evolved into
a serious passion for playing the
guitar. He would spend countless
hours teaching himself how to play,
practicing until he could replicate the
riffs of his favorite rock songs. His
initial interest in rock music led him to
explore songwriting, and soon he
began to write his songs. This was the
beginning of Austin's journey as a
creator where he started to mold his
style, combining various musical
influences.
Austin's teenage years were also
marked by his deepening love for hip-
hop. Texas, particularly cities like
Houston, had a thriving rap scene, and

Austin was captivated by the sounds coming from artists like Paul Wall, Slim Thug and UGK. This Southern hip-hop influence, paired with his rock background, began to form the unique fusion that would later define his music. While most teenagers his age were content with just listening to their favorite artists, Austin was already thinking about how he could create his sound.

It was during these years that he adopted the stage name "Post Malone." The name "Post" came from his last name, and "Malone" was reportedly generated from a rap name generator online a humorous yet fitting start for an artist who would later dominate the music scene. This name would soon be associated with a sound that defied the conventions of the genre.

In high school, Austin's passion for music started to take precedence over other interests. Though he was involved in various activities, from sports to hanging out with friends, his focus remained on creating music. He formed a metal band with a few friends, tapping into his love for rock music, but it wasn't long before he turned his attention toward hip-hop and rap. His ability to shift between musical styles, even at this early stage, hinted at the genre-defying career that lay ahead.

The First Taste of Performing

Austin attended Grapevine High School, where he continued to immerse himself in music. It was during these years that he performed in front of crowds for the first time, though these performances were far from the packed arenas he would later command. He participated in local talent shows and performed with his band, giving him valuable experience on stage. These early performances were not only a way to build confidence but also to experiment with different musical styles in front of an audience.

Despite his growing passion for music, Austin's journey was not without its challenges. Like many aspiring artists, he faced skepticism and doubt from people who couldn't quite see his vision. His genre-blurring style, mixing rock with rap and pop, wasn't always understood by those around him. But Austin remained steadfast in his belief that he could make it in the music industry. His determination to succeed, combined with his natural talent, began to set him apart from his peers.

Creating a SoundCloud Presence

It was also during his high school years that Austin began to seriously consider pursuing music as a career. He started recording his songs and uploading them to SoundCloud, a platform that allowed independent artists to share their music with the world. This was a pivotal moment in his life. While SoundCloud has been the launching pad for many successful artists, it requires persistence and talent to stand out in a sea of uploads. Austin's willingness to put himself out there to share his music with the world demonstrated his commitment to his craft.

Though his early SoundCloud uploads didn't gain massive attention, they were the first step in building his online presence. It allowed him to receive feedback and refine his style, helping him understand what worked and what didn't. More importantly, it provided Austin with a platform to experiment with his sound, to mix and blend genres without the constraints of a record label or commercial expectations.

By the time he graduated high school, Austin was more determined than ever to pursue a music career. The success of uploading music online and his growing confidence as a performer gave him the push he needed to take the next step.

After High School: The Big Decision

After high school, Austin attended Tarrant County College for a brief time, but it was clear that his heart wasn't in it. Like many aspiring musicians, he faced a difficult choice: continue down the traditional path of education, or take a risk and pursue his passion full-time. In the end, Austin chose the latter. He dropped out of college after just a few months, betting on himself and his music career.

This decision would soon prove to be the right one. Leaving college allowed Austin to focus entirely on his music, setting the stage for what would become a life-changing move to Los

Angeles. Armed with his guitar, his
SoundCloud uploads, and an
unwavering belief in his potential,
Austin was ready to take the music
world by storm.

-

CHAPTER 3: THE FIRST BREAKTHROUGH: "WHITE IVERSON"

Recording and Releasing the Song
In 2015, Post Malone was still an
unknown artist, trying to make a name
for himself in the competitive music
industry. After moving to Los Angeles
with his longtime friend Jason Probst,
he was living in a shared house with
several aspiring musicians and video
game streamers. It was during this
time that Post Malone wrote and
recorded a track that would change his
life forever "White Iverson."
"White Iverson" was not just another
song it was a statement. Named after
NBA legend Allen Iverson, it
symbolized Post Malone's belief in
himself and his journey toward
greatness. He wrote the song in two
days, drawing inspiration from

basketball culture and his own experiences. The lyrics reflected themes of success, self-confidence, and ambition, all set against a smooth, laid-back beat that blended hip-hop with melodic undertones. This fusion of styles gave the song a unique edge, distinguishing it from other music in the hip-hop scene at the time.

Post Malone uploaded "White Iverson" to SoundCloud in February 2015, a decision that would prove to be a turning point in his career. At the time, he had no major label backing, no manager, and no major promotional push. But within days, the song started gaining traction online. It quickly racked up thousands of plays on SoundCloud, catching the attention of listeners who were captivated by Post Malone's distinctive voice and the song's catchy hook. The internet had discovered a new star, and Post Malone's rise had officially begun.

The Viral Success and Music Industry Attention

As "White Iverson" continued to spread across SoundCloud, its success began to snowball. Within a few months, the track had amassed millions of plays, and Post Malone was no longer just another aspiring artist in Los Angeles—he was becoming a sensation. The song's infectious melody and relatable lyrics resonated with a wide audience, from hip-hop fans to those who enjoyed pop and even rock influences. This cross-genre appeal was one of the key reasons for its success, setting Post Malone apart in an industry that often favored categorization.

The viral success of "White Iverson" also attracted the attention of record labels and industry insiders. In the music business, a viral hit can often serve as a launchpad for an artist's career, and Post Malone was no exception. Major labels quickly took notice of the young artist who had managed to achieve millions of streams with no formal support. Soon, he found himself in meetings with top executives, all eager to sign him to their label.

One of the industry veterans who noticed Post Malone's potential was Republic Records. Known for signing artists who break the mold, Republic recognized that Post Malone's genre-blending sound could resonate with a diverse audience. In August 2015, just six months after the release of "White Iverson," Post Malone signed a recording contract with Republic Records. This deal would mark the beginning of his journey into mainstream stardom.

What Made "White Iverson" Stand Out

The success of "White Iverson" wasn't just about its catchy beat or its basketball references. The song captured something deeper the mood and aspirations of a generation. At a time when hip-hop was evolving, with artists experimenting with more melodic and emotional sounds, Post Malone's approach felt fresh and authentic. His ability to blend genres mixing hip-hop with elements of R&B, pop, and rock gave the track a wide appeal. Unlike many artists, who stick to a single genre, Post Malone refused to be put in a box.

"White Iverson" also demonstrated Post Malone's talent for creating memorable hooks. The song's chorus, "When I started ballin', I was young," became an anthem for those chasing their dreams. The track wasn't just about basketball; it was about striving for success and overcoming obstacles, themes that resonated with many listeners.

Visually, Post Malone also made a significant impression. The music video for "White Iverson," released in July 2015, further cemented his unique identity. The video, shot in a desert landscape, featured Post Malone with his signature braids, gold grill, and tattoos, portraying an image that was both unconventional and intriguing. The video accumulated millions of views, helping to solidify his growing fan base.

The Challenges of Overnight Fame

While "White Iverson" brought Post Malone unprecedented attention and success, it also introduced new challenges. Almost overnight, he went from being an aspiring artist to a public figure, with all the pressures and scrutiny that came with fame. Some critics questioned whether Post Malone was just another one-hit-wonder, while others debated whether he fit into the hip-hop genre at all, given his rock influences and unconventional image.

Despite these criticisms, Post Malone remained focused on his music. He knew that "White Iverson" was just the beginning, and he was determined to prove that he was more than a viral sensation. His work ethic, combined with his ability to connect with a wide audience, helped him navigate the pressures of newfound fame.

Post Malone's early success also brought collaborations with major artists and producers. After signing with Republic Records, he began working with some of the biggest names in the music industry, including Kanye West and Justin Bieber. These collaborations helped expand his reach and further establish him as a rising star. Post Malone even went on tour with Justin Bieber in 2016, performing as the opening act on Bieber's Purpose World Tour, which introduced him to a global audience.

A New Era Begins

With "White Iverson," Post Malone had officially arrived on the music scene, but he knew he couldn't rest on his laurels. The success of the track opened doors for him, but it also set high expectations for his future work. Fans and critics alike were eager to see whether he could replicate the success of his breakout hit.

As Post Malone prepared to release his debut album, the music world watched closely. Would he be able to follow up "White Iverson" with more hits, or would he fade away like many viral sensations before him? Post Malone was ready to prove that he was here to stay.

CHAPTER 4: SIGNING WITH REPUBLIC RECORDS

Meeting Record Label Executives The viral success of "White Iverson" catapulted Post Malone into the spotlight, attracting attention from music executives across the industry. By mid-2015, the buzz surrounding Post Malone was undeniable, and several record labels were vying for a chance to sign the young artist. At the forefront of these companies was Republic Records, a label known for fostering unique and genre-defying talents. Home to a diverse roster of artists such as Drake, The Weeknd, and Ariana Grande, Republic Records seemed like the perfect fit for an artist like Post Malone, who didn't fit neatly into any single musical category.

The journey from uploading songs on SoundCloud to sitting in meetings with industry heavyweights was surreal for Post Malone. He was a young artist with a distinctive sound, but at this point, he had no formal music education or industry connections. What he did have, however, was an undeniable talent and a viral hit that showed he could connect with a broad audience.

Post Malone met with several executives, but Republic Records stood out because they understood his vision. Rather than trying to pigeonhole him into a specific genre or mold him into a typical pop star, Republic saw the potential in his genre-blending style. They recognized that Post Malone's ability to mix hip-hop, rock, pop, and even country influences was not just a novelty it was a reflection of the future of music.

In August 2015, Post Malone signed a recording contract with Republic Records. This deal marked a turning point in his career. Not only did it provide him with the resources and support to continue developing his music, but it also gave him access to a wide range of collaborators, producers, and opportunities that would help elevate his career to new heights.

Working with Producers and Collaborators

Once signed to Republic Records, Post Malone was thrust into the world of professional music production. The label paired him with top-tier producers and collaborators to help him refine his sound and create new music that would resonate with a global audience. For Post Malone, this was a dream come true. He had always been passionate about making music, but now he had the chance to work with some of the best in the industry. One of the first major producers he worked with was Louis Bell, a producer and songwriter who would become a key figure in Post Malone's career. Bell had an extensive background in pop and R&B, but he was also known for his versatility, which made him the perfect collaborator for Post Malone's genre-bending style. Together, they began working on what would become Post Malone's debut album, Stoney. Their partnership proved to be a winning combination, with Bell helping to shape Post Malone's sound while also allowing him the creative freedom to explore different musical directions. Another important collaborator for Post Malone during this time was FKi 1st, a producer who had worked with artists like Travis Scott and 2 Chainz. FKi 1st co-produced "White Iverson" and continued to play a significant role in the development of Post Malone's early music. His production style, which blended trap beats with more melodic elements, meshed perfectly with Post Malone's vocal style, creating a sound that was both radio-friendly and innovative.

In addition to working with producers, Post Malone also began collaborating with other artists. His ability to effortlessly shift between genres made him an attractive collaborator for musicians from a variety of backgrounds. He formed connections with major figures in the music industry, including Kanye West, who

invited him to work on the track
"Fade" from West's album The Life of
Pablo. This collaboration with one of
the most influential artists in the world
helped further solidify Post Malone's
credibility as a rising star.

Adjusting to Life as a Signed Artist

Signing with a major label like
Republic Records came with both
opportunities and challenges. While
Post Malone was now positioned to
reach a much larger audience, he also
had to adjust to the realities of being a
signed artist. He was no longer an
independent musician uploading songs
to SoundCloud he had deadlines to
meet, contracts to fulfill, and a
growing fanbase to satisfy. This
transition wasn't always easy,
especially for an artist as
unconventional as Post Malone, who
valued creative freedom above all else.
Despite these challenges, Post Malone
remained true to his artistic vision.
Republic Records allowed him the
freedom to experiment with his sound,
recognizing that his ability to blend
genres was what made him special.
Post Malone wasn't interested in

following trends or conforming to industry expectations he wanted to carve out his path. His focus was on making music that felt authentic to him, even if it didn't always fit neatly into established categories.

As a newly signed artist, Post Malone also began navigating the demands of touring and performing. With "White Iverson" still riding high on the charts, he started performing at various venues and music festivals, introducing his music to live audiences. These performances helped him build a loyal fanbase, many of whom were drawn to his laid-back, relatable persona as much as his music. Post Malone's ability to connect with fans on a personal level would become one of the defining features of his career.

A Balancing Act

While Post Malone was excited about his newfound success, he was also mindful of the need to balance his commercial ambitions with his happiness. Fame had come quickly, and with it came the pressures of being in the public eye. Post Malone was never one to seek out the spotlight; in

fact, his easygoing, unassuming
personality often contrasted with the
larger-than-life image that many in the
music industry projected. Despite the
glitz and glamour of his new life, Post
Malone remained grounded, focused
on his music and his relationships with
those closest to him.

As he prepared to release his debut
album, Post Malone knew that the
expectations were high. "White
Iverson" had been a breakout hit, and
now fans and critics alike were eager
to see what he would deliver next. But
Post Malone wasn't interested in
replicating his past success. Instead, he
wanted to evolve, to push his sound in
new directions while staying true to
the genre-blurring style that had made
him a star.

Signing with Republic Records opened
up a world of possibilities for Post
Malone. He now had the resources and
platform to take his music to the next
level, and he was determined to make
the most of it. With a debut album on
the horizon and collaborations with
some of the biggest names in music
under his belt, Post Malone was ready
to prove that he was more than just a
viral sensation—he was a true artist
with staying power.

As he looked ahead to the release of Stoney, Post Malone knew that his journey was just beginning. He had already defied expectations by blending genres and creating a sound that was uniquely his own. Now, with the support of Republic Records, he was poised to become one of the most influential artists of his generation.

CHAPTER 5: "STONEY"- POST MALONE'S DEBUT ALBUM

With his record deal in place and a growing fanbase eagerly awaiting his next move, Post Malone began working on his debut album, Stoney. Released in December 2016, Stoney was a highly anticipated project, as it would either cement Post Malone's status as a rising star or determine if he would fall into the category of one-hit wonders. The pressure was high, but Post Malone approached the project with the same laid-back demeanor that had endeared him to fans from the start.

The creation of Stoney was a process marked by collaboration, experimentation, and a clear desire to stay true to his artistic vision. Post Malone continued working closely with Louis Bell, who had played a crucial role in shaping his sound. Bell's production expertise helped refine Post Malone's genre-blending approach, while still allowing the music to feel raw and authentic. The goal was to make an album that could appeal to a wide audience without sacrificing the elements that made Post Malone unique.

One of the key challenges Post Malone faced while creating Stoney was balancing his various musical influences. He didn't want to be confined to one genre, and Stoney was designed to reflect that. The album mixed elements of hip-hop, R&B, pop, and rock, creating a sound that was difficult to categorize but undeniably catchy. The lyrical themes of the album were also diverse, ranging from love and heartbreak to success and personal growth. This blend of sounds and themes ensured that Stoney resonated with listeners from different musical backgrounds.

In addition to Bell, Post Malone worked with other producers and songwriters to bring his vision to life.

FKi 1st, who had co-produced "White Iverson", continued to collaborate with Post Malone on several tracks, further enhancing the album's unique sound. While Post Malone was still relatively new to the industry, he was clear about what he wanted, and his collaborators helped him bring his ideas to fruition.

Reception and Breakout Hits Like "Congratulations"

When Stoney was released in December 2016, the response was overwhelmingly positive. Fans who had been following Post Malone since "White Iverson" were thrilled to see that he had delivered a full-length project that lived up to the hype. The album debuted at number six on the Billboard 200 chart, a remarkable achievement for a debut artist. Critics, too, praised Stoney for its genre-defying sound and Post Malone's ability to fuse hip-hop with other musical styles in a way that felt fresh and original.

The breakout hit from Stoney was undoubtedly "Congratulations," featuring rapper Quavo of Migos.

Released as a single shortly before the album, "Congratulations" became an instant anthem for success and perseverance. The track's celebratory tone, coupled with its infectious chorus, made it a favorite for fans and quickly turned into one of Post Malone's signature songs. The lyrics of "Congratulations" encapsulated Post Malone's journey from obscurity to stardom, with lines like "Now they always say congratulations, worked so hard, forgot how to vacation" reflecting his newfound success. "Congratulations" also marked Post Malone's first major collaboration with a prominent figure in the rap world. Quavo's verse added an extra layer of appeal to the track, bridging the gap between Post Malone's genre-blending style and mainstream hip-hop. The song's success was further boosted by a music video that featured lavish visuals of celebration and achievement, solidifying Post Malone's image as an artist who had made it.

"Congratulations" went on to become one of the most successful singles of Post Malone's career. It peaked at number eight on the Billboard Hot 100 chart and was eventually certified

Diamond by the Recording Industry
Association of America (RIAA),
signifying over 10 million units sold.
The song's success helped propel
Stoney to even greater heights,
ensuring that Post Malone's debut
album would be remembered as one of
the defining projects of his career.
In addition to "Congratulations",
Stoney featured other standout tracks
that helped solidify Post Malone's
place in the music industry. Songs like
"Go Flex", "Deja Vu" (featuring Justin
Bieber), and "I Fall Apart" showcased
Post Malone's versatility as an artist.
"Go Flex" combined acoustic guitar
with trap beats, creating a unique
blend of rock and hip-hop that
reflected Post Malone's genre-bending
approach. Meanwhile, "Deja Vu"
brought in pop elements, thanks in part
to Bieber's feature, and "I Fall Apart"
displayed Post Malone's emotional
depth, touching on themes of
heartbreak and vulnerability.

Post Malone's Breakout Moment

While "White Iverson" had introduced
Post Malone to the world, Stoney
solidified his status as a major player

in the music industry. The album's success proved that Post Malone was more than just a viral sensation he was an artist with staying power and a unique voice in an increasingly saturated music scene. With Stoney, Post Malone had successfully navigated the tricky transition from internet fame to mainstream success, and he had done so on his terms. One of the reasons for Stoney's enduring success was its ability to appeal to a broad range of listeners. Post Malone's refusal to stick to one genre meant that his music resonated with fans of hip-hop, pop, and rock alike. This versatility made Stoney a standout project in a time when many artists were sticking to the confines of a single genre. Post Malone's approach felt refreshing, and it spoke to a generation of listeners who were increasingly uninterested in labels and boundaries in music.

The success of Stoney also established Post Malone as a figure who could not be easily categorized. His image complete with face tattoos, gold teeth, and a laid-back, often disheveled appearance was unconventional, but it resonated with fans who appreciated his authenticity.

Post Malone wasn't trying to fit into any particular mold, and that sense of individuality was reflected in both his music and his persona.

Legacy of "Stoney"

In the years since its release, Stoney has continued to enjoy massive success. The album has been streamed billions of times across platforms and has remained a fan favorite, particularly among those who appreciate Post Malone's ability to blur the lines between genres. Stoney was eventually certified quadruple platinum by the RIAA, further cementing its place as one of the most successful debut albums in recent memory. Post Malone's debut album also laid the foundation for what would come next. Stoney introduced the world to his unique sound, but it was clear that Post Malone was just getting started. His ability to experiment with different styles and create music that was both commercially successful and artistically innovative set him apart from many of his peers. As he prepared to work on his second album, Beerbongs & Bentleys, Post Malone had established himself as one of the most exciting and unpredictable artists in the music world.

With Stoney, Post Malone had proven that he was more than just a viral sensation; he was a true artist with the potential to shape the future of music.

CHAPTER 6: THE EVOLUTION OF SOUND: "BEERBONGS & BENTLEYS"

A Look at the Themes and Production of the Second Album.

Following the massive success of his debut album, Stoney, Post Malone faced the daunting task of crafting a sophomore effort that could live up to the high expectations set by his initial release. He began working on his second studio album, Beerbongs & Bentleys, to further evolve his sound while still retaining the authenticity that had garnered him a dedicated fanbase. Released in April 2018, Beerbongs & Bentleys showcased Post Malone's growth as an artist, both musically and thematically.

The album title itself, Beerbongs & Bentleys, was a reflection of the lifestyle that had come to be associated with Post Malone. It encapsulated the duality of indulgence and luxury, juxtaposing the carefree party lifestyle with the more serious themes that often ran through his music. As with Stoney, Post Malone continued to blend genres, but this time he incorporated even more eclectic influences, ranging from hip-hop and pop to rock and country, making the album a rich tapestry of sounds.

Post Malone's collaborators on Beerbongs & Bentleys were key to the album's production. He once again teamed up with producer Louis Bell, who had become a close creative partner. Bell's production style characterized by his ability to seamlessly blend different genres perfectly complemented Post Malone's artistic vision. They also brought in other notable producers and artists to enhance the album's sound. The combination of talents created a dynamic atmosphere, allowing for experimentation while maintaining Post Malone's signature style.

Chart-topping hits Like "Rockstar" and "Psycho"

Beerbongs & Bentleys was met with overwhelming anticipation, and it did not disappoint. The album debuted at number one on the Billboard 200 chart and broke several streaming records upon its release. Its lead single, "Rockstar", featuring 21 Savage, became a cultural phenomenon. The track captured the essence of the rockstar lifestyle, blending trap beats with catchy melodies and introspective lyrics about fame, success, and the accompanying pressures.

"Rockstar" was not only a commercial success; it also showcased Post Malone's ability to write lyrics that resonated with listeners. The song's themes of excess and the pitfalls of fame reflected Post Malone's own experiences in the spotlight. It quickly climbed to the top of the charts, reaching number one on the Billboard Hot 100, and it maintained that position for eight consecutive weeks. The music video, featuring Post Malone in various extravagant settings, further cemented his image as a modern rockstar, complete with the lavish lifestyle that came with his fame.

Another significant hit from Beerbongs & Bentleys was "Psycho," featuring Ty Dolla $ign. This track continued the trend of blending melodic hooks with rap influences, showcasing Post Malone's signature sound. "Psycho" also found commercial success, reaching the top ten of the Billboard Hot 100 and showcasing Post Malone's ability to create infectious tracks that resonated with a wide audience.

The album was packed with other standout tracks, such as "Better Now," which dealt with themes of heartbreak and loss, and "Ball for Me," featuring Nicki Minaj, which explored the juxtaposition of success and personal struggles. Each song on Beerbongs & Bentleys contributed to the album's narrative, painting a vivid picture of Post Malone's life, experiences, and evolution as an artist.

A Bold Musical Direction

With Beerbongs & Bentleys, Post Malone took bold steps in his musical direction. While Stoney had already established his genre-blurring style, this album saw him embracing more experimental sounds and lyrics. He incorporated elements of rock, pop-punk, and even country, showcasing his versatility and willingness to push boundaries. The use of live instrumentation and diverse musical arrangements also marked a noticeable shift from the more digital production of Stoney.

Post Malone's lyrical themes matured as well. While Stoney often touched on the excitement of newfound fame and success, Beerbongs & Bentleys delved deeper into the complexities of that lifestyle. He explored the emotional toll of fame, the transient nature of relationships, and the darker side of the party scene. Songs like "I Fall Apart" and "Stay" highlighted his vulnerability, allowing listeners to connect with him on a more personal level.

Post Malone also became more comfortable with his unique blend of humor and introspection. His ability to juxtapose lighthearted elements with serious themes became a hallmark of his writing style. This combination resonated with fans, as it reflected the reality of navigating success in the modern age celebratory yet fraught with challenges.

Critical Reception and Commercial Success

Upon its release, Beerbongs & Bentleys received generally positive reviews from critics, who praised Post Malone's growth as an artist and his ability to create relatable yet aspirational music. The album was celebrated for its diversity and the seamless blend of genres, further solidifying Post Malone's reputation as a trailblazer in the music industry. Commercially, Beerbongs & Bentleys shattered records, becoming one of the most-streamed albums in a single week at the time of its release. It broke the record for the most simultaneous Hot 100 entries for a solo artist, showcasing the sheer volume of hits that had emerged from the album. This

level of success reaffirmed Post
Malone's status as one of the leading
figures in contemporary music.
With the success of Beerbongs &
Bentleys, Post Malone solidified his
position as a household name. He
became a mainstay on charts around
the world, and his songs became
anthems for a generation. The album's
impact was felt not only in the charts
but also in popular culture, as fans
embraced his music, style, and
persona.

The Legacy of "Beerbongs & Bentleys"

As time passed, the legacy of
Beerbongs & Bentleys only grew. The
album is often regarded as a defining
moment in Post Malone's career,
showcasing his evolution as an artist
and his ability to connect with a
diverse audience. It set the stage for
future projects and collaborations,
establishing him as a key player in the
ever-changing music landscape.
Beerbongs & Bentleys was more than
just an album; it was a cultural
moment that highlighted the shifting

dynamics in music. Post Malone's genre-blending approach and willingness to embrace his unique identity resonated with fans, paving the way for other artists to explore similar paths.

In the years following its release, the influence of Beerbongs & Bentleys continued to shape the industry. Post Malone's success inspired a new generation of musicians who sought to break free from traditional genre constraints. His ability to create hits while remaining authentic to his experiences became a blueprint for aspiring artists navigating the complexities of the music business.

As Post Malone moved forward in his career, Beerbongs & Bentleys remained a significant milestone, representing his growth as an artist and the impact he had made in a short period. With this album, he had proven that he was not just a flash in the pan but a true force to be reckoned with in the music world.

CHAPTER 7: POST MALONE'S UNIQUE STYLE AND PERSONA

Fashion, Tattoos, and His Distinctive Look

Post Malone's ascent to fame has been marked not only by his music but also by his striking personal style and distinctive persona. From the moment he entered the music scene, he stood out—not just for his catchy songs but for his unconventional appearance and approach to fashion. Post Malone's style reflects a blend of influences, merging elements from various genres and cultures while embracing a laid-back, often scruffy aesthetic.

One of the most recognizable aspects of Post Malone's look is his extensive collection of tattoos. His body art is not just for show; each tattoo holds personal significance and tells a part of his story. Post Malone's most prominent tattoos include the words "Always" and "Tired" inked under his eyes, which he has explained as a reminder of his commitment to authenticity and the constant challenges of fame. His tattoos often spark conversation, and he has become somewhat of a cultural icon for this bold expression of self.

Post Malone's fashion choices have contributed to his unique persona. He often embraces a mix of streetwear, high fashion, and vintage styles. You might see him in baggy graphic tees, oversized hoodies, or distressed jeans paired with statement sneakers. His wardrobe choices often reflect his personality unpretentious and relaxed, yet intentionally styled. Post Malone's style has resonated with fans who appreciate his ability to blend comfort with creativity, setting him apart from more traditionally polished pop stars. Post Malone's look is further accentuated by his playful approach to accessories. He often dons sunglasses, jewelry, and hats, adding to his laid-back rockstar image. This ability to mix high-end fashion with everyday wear has not only made him a trendsetter but also a relatable figure to many fans. He embraces the philosophy that fashion should be fun, which is evident in his various collaborations with fashion brands, allowing him to express his individuality further.

Blending Hip-Hop, Rock, and Pop: A Musical Pioneer

One of the most defining characteristics of Post Malone's career is his ability to blend multiple musical genres seamlessly. He emerged in an era where genre lines were becoming increasingly blurred, and his willingness to experiment with different styles has set him apart as a musical pioneer. Post Malone's sound encompasses elements of hip-hop, rock, pop, and even country, appealing to a diverse audience that transcends traditional genre boundaries.

His musical journey began with influences from various genres. Growing up, he was exposed to a wide range of music, from classic rock bands like Nirvana and Pink Floyd to hip-hop legends such as 50 Cent and Eminem. This eclectic mix of influences laid the foundation for his unique sound, allowing him to create music that feels fresh and innovative. Post Malone's ability to craft catchy hooks and memorable melodies has made his music universally appealing. Songs like "Rockstar" and "Circles" feature melodic choruses that draw in listeners from different backgrounds, while still maintaining a strong connection to hip-hop and rap. His vocal delivery often shifts between singing and rapping, showcasing his versatility and ability to navigate various musical styles.

In addition to his career, Post Malone has collaborated with a diverse array of artists, further highlighting his genre-blending approach.

Collaborations with rappers like 21 Savage and Ty Dolla $ign have anchored his hip-hop credentials, while partnerships with pop and rock artists, such as Justin Bieber and Ozzy Osbourne, showcase his willingness to experiment and push boundaries. His collaboration with Osbourne on the song "Take What You Want" marked a significant moment in his career, bridging the gap between rock and hip-hop while introducing his sound to a new audience.

The Connection with Fans: Relatability and Authenticity

What truly sets Post Malone apart is his relatability and authenticity. In an industry often filled with polished personas and curated images, Post

Malone embraces a more genuine approach. He often speaks candidly about his experiences, both the highs and the lows, allowing fans to connect with him on a personal level. His lyrics frequently reflect themes of vulnerability, heartbreak, and the struggles of navigating fame, resonating deeply with listeners who see their own experiences reflected in his music.

Post Malone's down-to-earth demeanor has endeared him to fans worldwide. He is known for his casual, unpretentious attitude, often appearing in simple clothing and being open about his love for beer and tattoos. This relatability has contributed to his massive popularity, as fans feel they can identify with him beyond the music. Post Malone's persona invites fans into his world, making them feel as if they are part of his journey.

Social media has played a significant role in shaping Post Malone's image. He often shares glimpses of his life, showcasing both the glamorous aspects of fame and the everyday moments that resonate with his audience. His playful interactions with fans, whether through humorous posts or spontaneous videos, create a sense of intimacy that draws people in. Post Malone is not just a musician; he is a friend, a relatable figure who invites fans to share in his life.

A New Kind of Rockstar

In many ways, Post Malone represents a new breed of rockstar one that doesn't conform to traditional expectations. He embodies the ethos of the modern artist who refuses to be boxed in by genre constraints or industry standards. Post Malone has created a space where he can be unapologetically himself, celebrating his individuality while still connecting with millions of fans worldwide.
His influence extends beyond music; Post Malone's unique style and persona have permeated popular culture. He has become a symbol of a generation that values authenticity over perfection and encourages self-expression in all its forms. As he continues to evolve as an artist, Post Malone's impact on the music industry and popular culture will undoubtedly leave a lasting legacy.

A Trailblazer for Future Generations

As Post Malone's career progresses, he remains committed to pushing boundaries and challenging the status quo. His genre-blending style and authentic persona have redefined what it means to be a successful artist in the modern age. He has opened the door for a new wave of musicians to explore their identities and express themselves without limitations.

Post Malone's unique style and ability to connect with fans through his music will continue to inspire future generations of artists. He has proven that success in the music industry doesn't have to fit a predetermined mold and that embracing one's individuality can lead to greatness. As he continues to forge his path, Post Malone stands as a testament to the power of authenticity, creativity, and the enduring impact of music in bringing people together.

CHAPTER 8:
"HOLLYWOOD'S

BLEEDING" AND CONTINUED SUCCESS

Exploring the Third Studio Album
After the monumental success of
Beerbongs & Bentleys, Post Malone
was faced with the challenge of
following up on an album that had
redefined his career and solidified his
place in the music industry. In
September 2019, he released his third
studio album, Hollywood's Bleeding,
which further showcased his evolution
as an artist while continuing to explore
themes of fame, love, and self-
reflection.

Hollywood's Bleeding is an album that
embodies the complexities of life in
the spotlight. The title itself reflects
Post Malone's recognition of the dual
nature of Hollywood—the allure and
the pitfalls of fame. Throughout the
album, he delves into his experiences
with success, the loneliness that can
accompany it, and the desire for
genuine connections amid the chaos of
celebrity life.

The production of Hollywood's
Bleeding maintained the genre-
blending approach that Post Malone
had become known for, incorporating

elements of hip-hop, rock, pop, and even country. Collaborating with a range of talented producers, including Louis Bell, Andrew Watt, and Frank Dukes, Post Malone was able to create a sound that felt both cohesive and diverse. The album's production features rich instrumentation, melodic hooks, and a variety of beats that cater to different musical tastes, ensuring that it appeals to a wide audience.

Chart-Topping Hits and Collaborations

Upon its release, Hollywood's Bleeding debuted at number one on the Billboard 200 chart, marking Post Malone's third consecutive album to achieve this feat. The lead single, "Wow," quickly became a commercial success, reaching the top ten of the Billboard Hot 100 and showcasing Post Malone's knack for creating infectious tracks that resonate with listeners. The song's catchy hook and upbeat production made it a favorite among fans and further solidified Post Malone's status as a pop culture icon. Another standout track from the album was "Circles," which showcased a more introspective side of Post

Malone. This song delved into themes of love and heartbreak, combining heartfelt lyrics with a melodic and catchy chorus. "Circles" received critical acclaim and commercial success, becoming one of Post Malone's most significant hits. The track reached number one on the Billboard Hot 100 and showcased his ability to blend emotional depth with mainstream appeal.

Post Malone also collaborated with several notable artists on Hollywood's Bleeding, including Halsey and SZA. The track "Die For Me," featuring Halsey and Future, explored themes of betrayal and loss, with each artist bringing their unique sound and perspective to the song. The collaboration highlighted Post Malone's willingness to experiment and push boundaries, as he continued to forge relationships with artists from different genres.

The album also features the song "Goodbyes," which features rapper Young Thug. This collaboration further emphasizes Post Malone's versatility and ability to navigate various musical landscapes. The emotional weight of the song, combined with its catchy melody,

resonated with fans and became
another hit from the album.

Critical Reception and Impact

Critically, Hollywood's Bleeding
received generally positive reviews,
with many praising Post Malone's
growth as an artist and his ability to
articulate the complexities of fame and
personal relationships. Critics noted
that the album felt more cohesive than
his previous work, showcasing a
maturity in both production and
songwriting. Post Malone's
willingness to explore deeper
emotional themes set Hollywood's
Bleeding apart from many other
albums in the pop and hip-hop genres.
The album's success was also reflected
in its performance on various music
charts. In addition to debuting at
number one on the Billboard 200,
Hollywood's Bleeding also achieved
significant success on global charts,
further solidifying Post Malone's status
as a worldwide superstar. The album
was certified multi-platinum by the
RIAA, a testament to its commercial
impact and popularity among fans.

Beyond commercial success, Hollywood's Bleeding contributed to the ongoing conversation about mental health and the realities of fame in the music industry. Post Malone's candid lyrics about his struggles with loneliness and the pressures of celebrity life resonated with listeners who appreciated his authenticity. By addressing these themes, he continued to foster a sense of connection with his audience, proving that even during success, he remained grounded and relatable.

Post Malone's Continued Evolution

With the release of Hollywood's Bleeding, Post Malone demonstrated that he was not content to rest on his laurels. He was committed to pushing the boundaries of his sound and exploring new artistic directions. The album served as a reflection of his growth as both an artist and an individual, as he navigated the challenges of fame while staying true to himself.

Post Malone's evolution extended beyond music; he also began to embrace his role as a cultural icon. His unique style, authenticity, and willingness to tackle difficult subjects in his lyrics resonated with fans and set him apart from many of his contemporaries. He became a figure who represented the complexities of modern life, combining elements of vulnerability and strength in his music. As Hollywood's Bleeding continued to gain traction, Post Malone remained active in his personal and professional life. He engaged with fans on social media, sharing glimpses of his life and showcasing his love for art, gaming, and collaboration. His commitment to staying connected with his audience only deepened their appreciation for him, solidifying his position as a beloved artist in the industry.

The Future of Post Malone

Looking ahead, Post Malone's trajectory seemed poised for continued success. With each album release, he demonstrated a willingness to evolve and experiment, ensuring that his music remained fresh and relevant. The themes explored in Hollywood's Bleeding provided a glimpse into his experiences, and fans eagerly anticipated what he would explore next.

Post Malone's impact on the music industry was undeniable. He had redefined what it meant to be a modern rockstar, combining elements of various genres while staying true to his identity. His ability to connect with fans on a personal level set him apart, and his music resonated with listeners across the globe.

As Post Malone continued to navigate the complexities of fame, he remained dedicated to his craft and his fans. With a commitment to authenticity and creativity, he was ready to embark on new musical journeys and explore fresh artistic directions. The legacy of Hollywood's Bleeding would undoubtedly serve as a significant chapter in his ongoing story, but it was clear that Post Malone had only just begun to make his mark on the music world.

CHAPTER 9: AWARDS AND ACCOLADES

Grammy Nominations and Wins
Post Malone's ascent in the music industry has not only been marked by

commercial success but also by critical recognition and numerous accolades. From the moment he burst onto the scene with White Iverson, it was clear that he possessed a unique talent that would resonate with audiences. His ability to blend genres and create infectious melodies quickly garnered the attention of music critics and industry professionals alike, leading to a slew of nominations and awards. One of the most prestigious accolades that Post Malone has pursued throughout his career is the Grammy Award. His first nomination came in 2018 when he was recognized for his debut album Stoney. The album received a nomination for Best Rap/Sung Performance for the hit single "Congratulations," which featured Quavo from Migos. This nomination marked a significant milestone for Post Malone, as it was a validation of his talent and the impact of his music within the industry. The following year, Post Malone's sophomore album, Beerbongs & Bentleys, was nominated for Album of the Year and Best Pop Vocal Album at the 61st Annual Grammy Awards. The album was celebrated for its genre-blending sound and commercial success, making it a formidable contender in several categories. The lead single "Rockstar," featuring 21 Savage, also earned a nomination for Record of the Year and Best Rap/Sung Performance. Though he did not take home a Grammy that year, the nominations solidified his standing as one of the leading artists of his generation.

In 2020, with the release of Hollywood's Bleeding, Post Malone received even more recognition. The album earned him nominations for Best Pop Solo Performance for the hit single "Circles" and Best Rap/Sung Performance for "Sunflower," a collaboration with Swae Lee for the Spider-Man: Into the Spider-Verse soundtrack. Sunflower became a cultural phenomenon, capturing the hearts of fans and critics alike, and the nominations reflected Post Malone's continued relevance in the industry. While Post Malone has yet to win a Grammy, his multiple nominations illustrate the significant impact he has made on modern music. His ability to create chart-topping hits that resonate with a diverse audience speaks volumes about his talent and artistry. Post Malone's dedication to his craft and his commitment to exploring new sounds and themes has ensured that he remains a prominent figure in the industry.

Recognition Across Various Music Platforms

In addition to Grammy nominations, Post Malone has received accolades from various music platforms, highlighting his influence and success in the industry. At the Billboard Music Awards, he has been a dominant force, winning several awards across multiple categories. Post Malone has been recognized as a Top Artist, Top Male Artist, and Top Streaming Songs Artist, among others.

His song "Rockstar" won Top Rap Song and Top Streaming Song at the Billboard Music Awards, further establishing its status as a cultural milestone. The song's success was a testament to Post Malone's ability to create music that resonates with fans and transcends genre boundaries. His impressive performance at the Billboard Music Awards, where he delivered a captivating rendition of

"Rockstar," showcased his prowess as a live performer and further endeared him to fans.

The American Music Awards have also recognized Post Malone's impact on the music scene. He won the award for Favorite Soul/R&B Male Artist and was nominated for Favorite Pop/Rock Male Artist, illustrating his versatility and broad appeal across genres. His wins at the American Music Awards reflect the admiration and support of fans who appreciate his contributions to the music industry. Additionally, Post Malone's achievements extend to the iHeartRadio Music Awards, where he has won awards for Song of the Year and Best New Artist. These accolades further demonstrate his growing influence and popularity in the music landscape.

Cultural Impact and Influence

Beyond the awards and nominations, Post Malone's cultural impact is undeniable. He has become a defining figure for a new generation of musicians, inspiring countless artists to explore genre-blending and self-expression in their work. His authenticity and willingness to embrace his individuality have resonated with fans, creating a strong connection that goes beyond just music.

Post Malone's presence in popular culture has also been amplified by his appearances in various media and collaborations with other artists. His features in high-profile music festivals and award shows have solidified his status as a mainstream artist. He has appeared on platforms like Saturday Night Live and The Tonight Show Starring Jimmy Fallon, showcasing his charisma and engaging stage presence. Post Malone's collaborations with a diverse range of artists have expanded his reach and influence. Working with artists from different genres allows him to bridge gaps and bring together fans from various musical backgrounds. His ability to collaborate successfully has made him a sought-after partner in the industry, leading to memorable tracks that resonate with listeners.

Post Malone's influence extends to fashion and lifestyle as well. His distinctive style and relaxed persona have inspired trends in streetwear and casual fashion, leading to collaborations with brands that align with his aesthetic. He has embraced partnerships that reflect his love for art and creativity, allowing him to express himself beyond the music realm.

Building a Lasting Legacy

As Post Malone continues to navigate his career, the accolades and recognition he has received only add to his growing legacy. His contributions to the music industry and his impact on popular culture have positioned him as one of the most influential artists of his generation. The awards and nominations he has received serve as a testament to his hard work, talent, and dedication to his craft.

Looking to the future, Post Malone's journey is far from over. With each new project, he has the opportunity to redefine himself and push the boundaries of his artistry. The road ahead holds immense potential for further exploration and innovation, and fans eagerly anticipate what he will create next.

Post Malone's story is one of resilience, creativity, and the pursuit of authenticity. As he continues to evolve and inspire, his influence on the music industry and popular culture will undoubtedly leave a lasting mark. Whether he receives awards or not, his legacy is built on the connections he has made with fans, the boundaries he has pushed, and the music he has created. With each new chapter, Post Malone solidifies his place in the annals of music history.

CHAPTER 10: POST MALONE'S INFLUENCE ON POP CULTURE

Post Malone's rise to fame has coincided with a shift in the music landscape, where genre boundaries have become increasingly fluid. His unique blend of hip-hop, rock, and pop has not only redefined musical norms but has also established him as a significant cultural figure. As a modern-day rockstar, he has made indelible marks on music, fashion, and social media, influencing not just his contemporaries but also future generations of artists.

One of the most notable aspects of Post Malone's influence is his approach to music. By seamlessly blending genres, he has paved the way for a new wave of artists who feel empowered to explore various sounds without being confined to a specific category. Songs like "Rockstar" and "Circles" have shown that chart-topping hits can draw from diverse influences, encouraging musicians to experiment and innovate. This genre-blending approach has made him a pivotal figure in the evolution of contemporary music, inspiring others to adopt a more eclectic style.

Post Malone's impact extends beyond music to fashion. His distinctive style, characterized by a mix of streetwear and high fashion, has resonated with fans and inspired trends across various demographics. He often wears oversized tees, baggy pants, and statement sneakers, embodying a relaxed yet stylish aesthetic. This casual style, combined with his extensive tattoos and nonchalant demeanor, has redefined what it means to be a rockstar in the modern era. Fashion brands have taken notice of Post Malone's influence, resulting in collaborations that highlight his artistic vision. His partnerships with companies like Crocs and his brand of wine, Maison No. 9, showcase his willingness to step outside traditional music boundaries and venture into the lifestyle space. By merging his love for music with fashion and business, Post Malone has solidified his status as a multifaceted artist who embodies the spirit of his generation.

In the realm of social media, Post Malone has also made a significant impact. His authentic and relatable presence on platforms like Instagram, Twitter, and TikTok has endeared him to fans worldwide. He frequently shares glimpses of his life, music-making process, and personal moments, creating a sense of intimacy that fosters a connection with his audience. This open approach has contributed to his massive following and has allowed fans to feel like they are part of his journey.

Collaborations with Other Artists

Post Malone's collaborations with a diverse array of artists have further amplified his influence in the music industry. His willingness to work with musicians from various genres—such as rock legends like Ozzy Osbourne, pop stars like Justin Bieber, and hip-hop artists like 21 Savage—has created memorable tracks that resonate with a broad audience. These collaborations not only showcase his versatility but also highlight the growing trend of genre-crossing in contemporary music.

For instance, his collaboration with Ozzy Osbourne on the song "Take What You Want" was a landmark moment, bridging the gap between rock and hip-hop. The track's success introduced Post Malone to rock fans while allowing Osbourne to reach a new generation of listeners. This kind of cross-pollination exemplifies how Post Malone is actively reshaping the musical landscape and creating opportunities for diverse artists to collaborate.

Additionally, Post Malone's features on tracks with artists from different genres have made him a sought-after collaborator. His ability to adapt his style while maintaining his unique sound has positioned him as a key figure in the industry, encouraging a more inclusive and collaborative atmosphere. This influence has opened

doors for emerging artists and set a
precedent for future collaborations
across genres.

Cultural Significance and Representation

Beyond his musical contributions, Post
Malone's influence is rooted in cultural
representation. He has become a
symbol of authenticity in a world often
dominated by curated images and
personas. His openness about mental
health struggles, personal experiences,
and the challenges of fame resonates
with fans who appreciate his
candidness. By sharing his
vulnerabilities, he has created a safe
space for others to express their
feelings and experiences.
Post Malone's representation extends
to his diverse fan base, which includes
people from various backgrounds and
demographics. His music appeals to a
wide audience, transcending traditional
genre divisions. This broad appeal
speaks to the changing landscape of
music consumption, where listeners
are increasingly drawn to authenticity
and relatable narratives over strict
genre labels.

In an era where social issues and personal struggles are at the forefront, Post Malone's music serves as a reflection of contemporary society. His willingness to address themes of loneliness, love, and the complexities of fame allows listeners to connect with him on a deeper level. This cultural significance has solidified his role as a voice for a generation, making him not just an artist but also an influential figure in the ongoing conversation about mental health and personal identity.

The Future of Post Malone's Influence

As Post Malone continues to evolve as an artist, his influence on pop culture is expected to grow even further. His commitment to authenticity, creativity, and collaboration will undoubtedly shape the music industry for years to come. With each new project, he has the opportunity to explore new themes, sounds, and artistic directions, keeping his music fresh and relevant.
Post Malone's ability to adapt to changing trends while staying true to himself will ensure that he remains a prominent figure in the industry. His

influence will likely inspire the next generation of artists to embrace their individuality, explore genre-blending, and connect with audiences on a personal level.

In a world where music often serves as a means of escape, Post Malone's authentic approach offers listeners a chance to engage with real emotions and experiences. His legacy will undoubtedly be defined by the connections he has made with fans, the boundaries he has pushed, and the lasting impact he has had on pop culture.

CHAPTER 11: PERSONAL LIFE

While Post Malone is best known for his musical talent and chart-topping hits, his personal life also plays a significant role in shaping who he is as an artist. Behind the scenes, he navigates the complexities of fame, relationships, and friendships, which contribute to his identity both on and off stage. Despite the glare of the spotlight, Post Malone has managed to maintain a sense of authenticity and connection to his roots.

Post Malone's relationships with family and friends are central to his life. He often speaks about the importance of his loved ones in keeping him grounded amid the chaos of fame. Raised in a supportive family, Post Malone's parents encouraged his artistic pursuits from a young age. His father, a former DJ, introduced him to various musical genres, fostering his passion for music. This strong familial bond has remained a cornerstone of his life, providing him with stability and love as he navigates the challenges of the industry.

Friendship is another critical aspect of Post Malone's personal life. He is known for surrounding himself with a close-knit group of friends, many of whom have been with him since his early days in the music scene. This sense of camaraderie is evident in his social media posts, where he often shares moments spent with friends, showcasing a genuine connection that goes beyond mere celebrity friendships. He values loyalty and authenticity, seeking out relationships that are built on mutual respect and understanding.

One notable friendship is with rapper and songwriter 21 Savage. The two first collaborated on the hit single "Rockstar," which became a defining track for both artists. Their friendship has since blossomed, with both supporting each other's careers and sharing personal moments. This bond reflects the kind of relationships Post Malone cherishes—ones that are built on trust and shared experiences in the industry.

Balancing Fame and Privacy

Despite his success, Post Malone has been vocal about the challenges of maintaining privacy in a world that constantly scrutinizes public figures. The relentless attention from fans and the media can make it difficult to navigate personal relationships and experiences. Post Malone has often expressed a desire to keep certain aspects of his life private, recognizing the importance of having a safe space away from the public eye.

He has taken steps to maintain that privacy, choosing to spend time in places where he feels comfortable and secure. For instance, Post Malone has expressed a preference for living outside of the traditional Hollywood scene, opting for a quieter life in his home in Utah. This decision allows him to find solace in nature and escape the pressures of celebrity culture. He has mentioned that spending time away from the spotlight helps him recharge and stay connected to what truly matters in life.

Post Malone's candidness about mental health struggles and the pressures of fame further emphasizes his desire to prioritize his well-being. He has openly discussed feeling overwhelmed at times, recognizing the importance of seeking help and support. This vulnerability not only humanizes him but also resonates with fans who appreciate his honesty. By sharing his experiences, Post Malone encourages conversations about mental health, fostering a sense of community among those who may be facing similar challenges.

The Role of Creativity in His Personal Life

Creativity is a significant aspect of Post Malone's life beyond his music career. He often engages in various artistic pursuits, including painting and designing. These creative outlets serve as a form of self-expression and a way for him to unwind from the pressures of fame. Post Malone has expressed a deep appreciation for art and has even showcased some of his work in galleries.

His love for creativity extends to his music-making process, where he often collaborates with other artists and producers. This collaborative spirit not only fuels his creativity but also allows him to build meaningful relationships within the industry. Working with like-minded individuals fosters an environment where ideas can flourish, resulting in innovative music that resonates with fans.

Post Malone's affinity for gaming is another aspect of his personal life that connects him to his fans. He has openly shared his passion for video games, often streaming his gameplay on platforms like Twitch. This engagement allows him to connect with his audience differently, showcasing his personality and interests outside of music. By sharing these moments, he reinforces the idea that he is relatable and grounded, just like his fans.

Navigating Fame with Authenticity

As Post Malone continues to rise in popularity, he remains committed to authenticity in his personal and professional life. He emphasizes the importance of staying true to oneself amid the pressures of fame. This authenticity is reflected in his music, where he explores real emotions and experiences that resonate with listeners.

Post Malone's approach to fame is characterized by a sense of humility. Despite his success, he often expresses gratitude for the opportunities he has received and acknowledges the support of his fans. This appreciation fosters a strong connection with his audience, who feel valued and recognized for their role in his journey.

Malone's personal life is a tapestry of relationships, creativity, and authenticity. His ability to navigate the complexities of fame while remaining true to himself is a testament to his character. By prioritizing his loved ones, mental health, and creative passions, Post Malone not only enriches his own life but also inspires others to embrace their individuality and pursue their passions.

CHAPTER 12: ENTREPRENEURIAL VENTURES

Post Malone's entrepreneurial spirit extends far beyond his musical career. As a multifaceted artist, he has ventured into various business opportunities that reflect his interests and personal brand. His ability to blend creativity with entrepreneurship has opened new avenues for growth and financial success, allowing him to diversify his portfolio while maintaining his authenticity.

One of Post Malone's most notable business ventures is his collaboration with the beverage industry. In 2020, he launched his line of rosé wine called Maison No. 9. Named after his favorite tarot card, the venture reflects his passion for wine and his desire to create a product that resonates with his fans. The wine has been well-received, quickly becoming a popular choice among consumers and showcasing

Post Malone's knack for branding and marketing.

Maison No. 9 is not just a product; it represents Post Malone's lifestyle and personal tastes. By entering the wine industry, he has positioned himself as more than just a musician he has become a lifestyle brand that embodies the spirit of celebration and enjoyment. His marketing strategy, which includes engaging social media campaigns and collaborations with influencers, has contributed to the wine's success, appealing to both his fans and wine enthusiasts alike.

Post Malone has also ventured into the world of merchandise. His unique style and persona have inspired a range of merchandise that resonates with fans. From clothing lines to accessories, Post Malone has capitalized on his image by creating products that reflect his artistic identity. Collaborations with established brands have allowed him to further expand his reach, creating exclusive collections that are highly sought after.

Passion for Beer: The Perfect Pairing

Post Malone's love for beer has also played a significant role in his entrepreneurial endeavors. He has openly expressed his appreciation for craft beer and has taken steps to develop his brand in the industry. In 2022, he partnered with the established beer brand Bud Light to create a limited-edition line of beer called "Posty." This collaboration not only aligns with his tastes but also reflects his ability to connect with fans through shared interests.

The "Posty" beer line showcases his commitment to quality and flavor, embodying the spirit of enjoyment that he promotes through his music. The branding and marketing strategies surrounding this venture are designed to create a sense of community among fans, inviting them to enjoy a cold beer while listening to Post Malone's hits. This approach highlights his understanding of how to engage with his audience beyond music, fostering a deeper connection through shared experiences.

Post Malone's love for beer and the brewing process has led him to explore opportunities to expand his footprint in the beverage industry further. He has expressed interest in developing unique flavors and collaborating with craft breweries to create limited-edition brews. By leveraging his influence and passion, he continues to carve out a niche for himself in the beverage market.

Innovative Collaborations and Artistic Expression

Post Malone's entrepreneurial ventures also reflect his commitment to artistic expression. He frequently collaborates with brands and artists to create unique products that resonate with his audience. These collaborations often blend music, art, and lifestyle, allowing him to showcase his creativity in new ways.

For example, Post Malone has partnered with the clothing brand Hyperfly to release a limited-edition line of apparel inspired by his music and personal style. This collaboration not only aligns with his artistic vision but also provides fans with an opportunity to connect with him through fashion. The success of such collaborations highlights his ability to navigate different industries while staying true to his brand.

Post Malone has ventured into the world of NFTs (non-fungible tokens), reflecting his interest in digital art and technology. By releasing limited-edition digital artwork and collectibles, he has embraced the growing trend of NFTs, appealing to a new generation of fans who appreciate the intersection of art and technology. This innovative approach showcases his willingness to explore new mediums and engage with fans in unique ways.

The Future of Post Malone's Entrepreneurial Journey

As Post Malone continues to evolve as an artist and entrepreneur, his ventures are likely to expand further. His keen business acumen and passion for creativity will undoubtedly lead to new opportunities that align with his brand. By exploring various industries, from music and fashion to beverages and digital art, he is establishing himself as a versatile entrepreneur with a lasting impact.

Post Malone's ability to blend his artistic identity with his business ventures will continue to resonate with fans and consumers alike. As he navigates the ever-changing landscape of entrepreneurship, his commitment to authenticity and creativity will serve as guiding principles. Whether through collaborations, product launches, or innovative marketing strategies, Post Malone's entrepreneurial journey is a testament to his multifaceted nature and enduring influence.

Post Malone's entrepreneurial ventures reflect his passion, creativity, and dedication to connecting with his audience. From his successful wine and beer brands to his innovative collaborations, he has carved out a unique space for himself in the business world. As he continues to explore new opportunities, fans eagerly anticipate the exciting ventures that lie ahead, knowing that Post Malone will always remain true to his artistic roots.

CHAPTER 13:
CHALLENGES AND
CONTROVERSIES

Handling Criticism and Media Scrutiny

As one of the most prominent figures in modern music, Post Malone has faced his share of challenges and controversies throughout his career. The pressures of fame can be overwhelming, and navigating the public's perception while remaining true to oneself is no easy feat. Despite his success, he has encountered criticism and scrutiny from the media and fans alike, which he has managed with a mix of grace and authenticity. One of the primary challenges Post Malone has faced is the constant scrutiny that comes with being a celebrity. From his fashion choices to his music, everything about him is often subject to analysis and critique. This level of attention can be daunting, and Post Malone has openly discussed the impact it has on his mental health. He has emphasized the importance of staying grounded and surrounding himself with supportive friends and family to cope with the pressures of fame.

Post Malone has also faced backlash for certain comments and actions that have sparked controversy. For instance, his remarks about hip-hop culture and the role of artists in the genre have sometimes led to misunderstandings and criticism from fans and fellow artists. He has expressed his love and respect for hip-hop while emphasizing that he draws inspiration from various musical genres, which may not always align with traditional hip-hop narratives. This nuanced perspective can sometimes be misinterpreted, leading to backlash from those who feel he is not fully embracing the genre's roots.

In response to criticism, Post Malone often takes a measured approach. He is known for his laid-back demeanor and reluctance to engage in public feuds or controversies. Instead of escalating conflicts, he tends to focus on his music and creative endeavors, demonstrating resilience in the face of negativity. This approach has garnered him respect from many fans who appreciate his authenticity and dedication to his craft.

Addressing Misunderstandings and Public Perception

One significant aspect of Post Malone's journey has been his efforts to address misunderstandings about his persona and artistry. In interviews, he has frequently discussed the importance of authenticity and staying true to oneself, highlighting the complexities of being an artist in the modern music landscape. He has emphasized that while he draws inspiration from various genres, his music is a reflection of his personal experiences and emotions.

Post Malone's willingness to engage in open conversations about his artistic intentions has helped clarify misconceptions surrounding his work. He often uses social media and interviews as platforms to express his thoughts, reinforcing the idea that his music transcends genre boundaries. By articulating his perspective, he fosters a deeper understanding of his artistry among fans and critics alike.

Post Malone has been candid about the impact of mental health on his life and career. He has shared his struggles with anxiety and the pressures of fame, emphasizing the importance of seeking help and being open about one's feelings. This vulnerability resonates with many fans who appreciate his honesty, as it encourages a more significant conversation about mental health within the music industry.

Navigating Personal Challenges

Beyond public scrutiny, Post Malone has faced personal challenges that have tested his resilience. The loss of loved ones, including the passing of friends and family members, has profoundly affected him. He often speaks about the importance of cherishing relationships and the impact of grief on his life. These experiences have shaped his outlook on life and influenced the themes present in his music.

Post Malone's journey has not been without its health challenges. He has experienced significant health issues, including a reported hospitalization in late 2022 due to exhaustion and dehydration after a rigorous tour schedule. This incident highlighted the importance of self-care and the need for artists to prioritize their well-being amidst the demands of the music industry. Post Malone has taken this experience as a reminder to listen to his body and take breaks when necessary, demonstrating a commitment to maintaining his health for the long haul.

The Impact of Controversies on His Career

Despite the challenges and controversies he has faced, Post Malone's career continues to thrive. His ability to address criticism and navigate personal struggles has not only endeared him to fans but has also reinforced his status as an influential figure in music. By maintaining his authenticity and staying true to his artistic vision, he has built a loyal fan base that appreciates his openness and relatability.

Post Malone's resilience is evident in his continued success and the evolution of his music. He has used past challenges as fuel for his creativity, resulting in songs that resonate deeply with listeners. His ability to transform adversity into artistic expression showcases his strength as an artist and his commitment to creating meaningful music.

As he moves forward in his career, Post Malone remains dedicated to his craft while staying true to himself. He understands that challenges and controversies are an inherent part of the journey, and he embraces them as opportunities for growth. His journey serves as an inspiration for aspiring artists and fans alike, illustrating the importance of perseverance, authenticity, and self-care.

Post Malone's challenges and controversies are integral to his story. His ability to navigate public scrutiny, address misunderstandings, and confront personal challenges has shaped him into the artist he is today. As he continues to evolve, he does so with resilience and authenticity, reminding us all that success is often accompanied by hurdles that can ultimately lead to greater growth and understanding.

CHAPTER 14: POST MALONE'S LEGACY

As Post Malone's career continues to flourish, discussions about his legacy and influence on music and culture have become increasingly prevalent. His ability to cross genres and create songs that resonate with a diverse audience has established him as a significant figure in modern music. However, the true measure of his legacy extends beyond chart-topping hits and record-breaking streams; it encompasses the lasting impact he has on future generations of artists and fans.

Post Malone's genre-blending approach has redefined the boundaries of contemporary music. By seamlessly integrating elements of hip-hop, rock, pop, and even country, he has demonstrated that music can be fluid and multifaceted. This innovative style encourages aspiring musicians to explore their own artistic identities without being confined to traditional genres. His success serves as a powerful example for those who wish to break free from genre constraints and experiment with their sound, fostering a new generation of artists willing to push creative boundaries. Post Malone's music often addresses universal themes such as love, heartbreak, and self-reflection. His lyrics resonate with listeners on a personal level, allowing fans to connect deeply with his experiences. This emotional authenticity encourages young artists to write from their perspectives and share their stories, fostering a culture of vulnerability and honesty in music. By paving the way for this type of expression, Post Malone has significantly influenced the lyrical landscape of contemporary music.

Reflection on His Contribution to Music and Culture

In addition to his musical impact, Post Malone's contribution to culture extends to his unique persona and approach to fame. He embodies a sense of relatability that resonates with fans, challenging the traditional image of a celebrity. Post Malone's laid-back demeanor, distinctive style, and candidness about mental health have endeared him to a generation that values authenticity and connection over the polished images often portrayed in the media.

His willingness to address personal struggles and vulnerabilities has opened the door for meaningful conversations about mental health within the music industry. As artists increasingly share their experiences, the stigma surrounding mental health issues is gradually diminishing. Post Malone's openness encourages fans to embrace their challenges and seek help when needed, fostering a culture of support and understanding.

His influence extends beyond music and mental health advocacy; he has made significant strides in promoting inclusivity and diversity in the industry. By collaborating with artists from various backgrounds and genres, he demonstrates the power of collaboration and unity in music. This commitment to inclusivity encourages young artists to embrace their identities and collaborate across boundaries, fostering a more diverse musical landscape.

A Lasting Impact on Pop Culture

Post Malone's impact on pop culture is evident in the way he has redefined what it means to be a modern rockstar. His style, characterized by tattoos, streetwear, and a laid-back attitude, resonates with fans who appreciate a more relatable and accessible persona. This departure from traditional celebrity norms has encouraged others to embrace their individuality and express themselves freely, creating a cultural shift that values authenticity over superficiality.

Post Malone's influence on social media and digital engagement has changed the way artists connect with their fans. His active presence on platforms like Instagram and TikTok allows him to share his personality and creativity in real time, fostering a deeper connection with his audience. This approach has set a new standard for artist-fan interactions, encouraging future musicians to engage with their fans in authentic and meaningful ways. As Post Malone continues to evolve as an artist, his legacy will undoubtedly grow. The foundations he has laid in music, mental health advocacy, inclusivity, and cultural representation will inspire future generations of artists and fans. His ability to break down barriers and connect with a diverse audience speaks to the power of music as a unifying force.

While it is still early in his career, Post Malone's legacy is already taking shape. As he explores new musical directions and expands his entrepreneurial ventures, the impact of his work will only continue to resonate. Future artists will look to him as a model of creativity, resilience, and authenticity, drawing inspiration from his journey.

Post Malone's ability to navigate the challenges of fame while remaining true to himself serves as a reminder that success is not solely defined by accolades but by the connections made and the lives touched along the way. His legacy will be measured not only by the music he creates but also by the positive influence he has on those who come after him.

Post Malone's legacy is a tapestry woven from his contributions to music, culture, and personal expression. His genre-blending approach, authenticity, and advocacy for mental health will leave an indelible mark on the industry and inspire future generations of artists to embrace their uniqueness and share their stories with the world. As Post Malone continues to innovate and evolve, his impact will be felt for years to come, solidifying his place as a cultural icon of our time.

CONCLUSION

In the ever-evolving landscape of modern music, Post Malone stands out as a defining figure of his generation. His journey from a young boy in Syracuse, New York, to a global superstar has been marked by resilience, creativity, and an unwavering commitment to authenticity. Throughout this biography, we have explored the various facets of Post Malone's life, from his early influences and breakthrough moments to the challenges and controversies that have shaped him into the artist he is today. Post Malone's impact on the music industry is undeniable. His unique ability to blend genres has redefined the boundaries of contemporary music, paving the way for future artists to explore their identities without being confined to traditional labels. By creating songs that resonate with fans on a personal level, he has fostered a culture of emotional honesty in music, encouraging artists to share their stories and experiences. This openness has transformed the way music is created and consumed, making it more relatable and accessible to a diverse audience.

Post Malone's contributions extend beyond his music. His candid discussions about mental health and personal struggles have sparked important conversations within the industry, encouraging both artists and fans to prioritize their well-being. By embodying vulnerability and resilience, he has become a beacon of hope for many, reminding them that it's okay to seek help and embrace their true selves.

Post Malone's influence on pop culture is profound. His laid-back persona and distinctive style have resonated with a generation that values authenticity and connection. He has challenged the traditional image of a rockstar, embracing individuality and encouraging others to do the same. As he continues to engage with fans through social media and various artistic ventures, he has redefined the relationship between artists and their audience, fostering a sense of community and shared experience.

As we look to the future, it is clear that Post Malone's legacy is just beginning to take shape. His entrepreneurial ventures, including his successful wine and beer brands, reflect his diverse interests and ability to innovate beyond music. By exploring new avenues of creativity, he is not only expanding his brand but also inspiring future generations of artists to embrace their multifaceted identities.

Post Malone's journey is a testament to the power of music as a unifying force. His ability to break down barriers, connect with diverse audiences, and inspire authenticity in others will leave a lasting impact on the industry and culture as a whole. As he continues to evolve and create, we can expect his influence to grow, solidifying his status as a cultural icon for years to come.

Post Malone's story is one of triumph, resilience, and artistic exploration. His contributions to music, culture, and mental health advocacy will resonate for generations, inspiring future artists to embrace their individuality and share their voices with the world. As we celebrate his achievements and look forward to what lies ahead, one thing is certain: Post Malone is not just a musician; he is a force of nature whose impact will be felt long into the future.

Made in the USA
Las Vegas, NV
18 December 2024

14699867R10056